NATURE'S ULTIMATE DISASTERS

TOP 10 WORST
FLOODS

Louise and Richard Spilsbury

PowerKiDS press
New York

Published in 2017 by
The Rosen Publishing Group, Inc.
29 East 21st Street, New York, NY 10010

Cataloging-in-Publication Data
Names: Spilsbury, Louise.
Title: Top 10 worst floods / Louise and Richard Spilsbury.
Description: New York : PowerKids Press, 2017. | Series: Nature's ultimate disasters | Includes index.
Identifiers: ISBN 9781499430738 (pbk.) | ISBN 9781499430752 (library bound) | ISBN 9781499430745 (6 pack)
Subjects: LCSH: Floods--Juvenile literature.
Classification: LCC GB1399.S65 2017 | DDC 363.34'93--dc23

Copyright © 2017 by The Rosen Publishing Group

Produced for Rosen by Calcium
Editors for Calcium Creative Ltd: Sarah Eason and Harriet McGregor
Designers: Paul Myerscough and Simon Borrough
Picture research: Rachel Blount

Picture credits: Cover: Dept of Defense: U.S. Coast Guard photograph by Petty Officer 2nd Class Kyle Niemi; Inside: NASA: Jacques Descloitres, MODIS Land Team 25; Shutterstock: Asianet-Pakistan 11, Paolo Costa 19c, Emattil 6–7, Sohel Parvez Haque 1, Jejim 23, Pius Lee 7, Dusan Milenkovic 4–5, Naveeen 17; Wikimedia Commons: Edu Alarcón 19t, Histed/Ernest Walter/1862-1947 13, Pieter Kuiper/Agency for International Development/National Archives 15, Leruswing 27, Archival Photography by Steve Nicklas, NOS, NGS 9, Airman 1st Class Cheryl Sanzi (USAF) 21.

All rights reserved. No part of this book may be reproduced in any form without permission in writing from the publisher, except by a reviewer.

Manufactured in the United States of America
CPSIA Compliance Information: Batch #BW17PK: For Further Information contact Rosen Publishing, New York, New York at 1-800-237-9932.

Contents

	Flood Danger	4
	Floods in Action	6
10	Mississippi	8
9	Pakistan	10
8	Johnstown	12
7	North Sea	14
6	North India	16
5	Venezuela	18
4	Bangladesh	20
3	Yangtze River	22
2	Ganges Delta	24
1	China	26
	Where in the World?	28
	Glossary	30
	Further Reading	31
	Index	32

FLOOD DANGER

When a flood brings water crashing onto land that is normally dry, it causes chaos. It can wash away people, cars, and trees, and bury homes under mud. It can ruin fields of crops and damage or destroy bridges and highways.

How Dangerous?

Some places experience small floods. Water from a river may overflow gently, washing only shallow water onto streets. Other floods are huge and last for weeks. The floodwaters can kill people, wash away possessions, knock down power lines, and cause fires. The dirt in floodwaters can also **pollute** drinking water supplies and cause disease.

Measuring Disaster

Scientists are trying to figure out how to predict floods and give people time to **evacuate** and reach higher ground or another safe place.

Floods happen when large clouds bring heavy rain. → People use **satellite** images taken from high above Earth's surface to see where rain clouds are heading.

Some clouds bring more rain than others. → Scientists use **radar** to detect how much moisture, or water droplets, there is in a cloud and whether it is in the form of rain or snow.

Floods happen when land cannot absorb water; for example, in areas of hard rock. → Scientists study land and make computer models and maps to show where floods are more likely to happen.

In 2014, heavy rains caused catastrophic flooding and mudslides, which destroyed the town of Krupanj in central Serbia.

Natural disasters have taken place since Earth was formed. People have many ways of deciding what the world's worst natural disasters have been, from the deadliest disaster to the costliest. This book includes some of the worst disasters in history.

FLOODS IN ACTION

Floods are one of the most common natural disasters in the world. They usually happen in places where flat, low-lying land meets rivers, lakes, or seas.

Rainwater washes more quickly down a slope without trees.

Rising Waters

When the level of the water in a river, lake, or sea rises, it can spill out over the land. Several things cause floods. Heavy rains can swell rivers. A storm can force seawater higher up the shore. **Cyclones** and **hurricanes** can bring sudden downpours, too, and earthquakes can cause large waves of water to wash onto the coast. Flash floods are floods that happen very suddenly after a huge rainstorm.

Where Floods Happen

Floods can happen almost anywhere. In places such as the United Kingdom, floods usually happen in the spring and fall seasons, when there is more rain. **Tropical** countries, such as India, have rainy and dry seasons. The **monsoon** season is when winds carrying moisture from the warm oceans nearby bring months of heavy rain. In these regions, there are regular and heavy floods during the monsoon season.

In some parts of the world, floods happen regularly and bring rainwater that is useful for growing crops such as rice.

Problems

People can sometimes increase the risk of flooding in an area. **Dams** and **reservoirs** are built to store water, but these can burst after prolonged, heavy rain and flood out onto towns and villages downstream. When people cut down forests, wind blows the top layer of earth away. Then, when it rains, the water runs off the land instead of soaking in. When people build highways and cover land in hard surfaces, there is even less soil to absorb rainwater.

10 MISSISSIPPI

The Great Mississippi Flood of 1927 is the biggest flood in US history and one of the worst ever natural disasters in the United States. It also became famous for the way some people in the worst-hit town, Greenville, treated the African Americans among them.

Mississippi

A River's Power

In 1927, in the Mississippi Valley, the rain came down in quantities that exceeded the yearly average by 10 or more times. Even though **tributaries** were overflowing, people in Greenville still felt safe because the US Army Corps of Engineers had built **levees** to keep back the Mississippi River. The engineers had assured people that the levees would hold. Unfortunately, everyone underestimated the river's power.

On the Record

African American **plantation** workers were forced to pile sandbags on top of the levees to reinforce them. When the levees broke, many workers were washed away and thousands were stranded for days without food or water.

The first levee broke on April 16, then another on April 21. Over the next few weeks, all the levees broke and collapsed, one after the other. Water poured through cracks and onto the streets.

It took more than two months for the floodwaters to completely subside.

In total, more than 23,000 square miles (60,000 sq km) of land was submerged, hundreds of thousands of people were made homeless, and around 250 people died.

In some places, homes were buried under 30 feet (9 m) of water. Tens of thousands of people were stranded on rooftops or left clinging to trees.

9 PAKISTAN

When the Indus River in Pakistan flooded in late July and early August 2010, it caused a terrible natural disaster that is considered to be one of the worst in the country's history.

Pakistan

Monsoon Floods

The floods were caused by record-breaking monsoon rains. Monsoon winds bring heavy rain to parts of Southeast Asia from May to September. They often cause floods but not usually on this scale. In 2010, the Indus River overflowed and broke through the flood defenses. The floodwaters washed away highways and bridges, and submerged large areas of land. Almost 2,000 people were killed.

On the Record

At its worst, the flood covered around one-fifth of Pakistan's land in water and affected almost 20 million people.

The floods damaged or destroyed 1.6 million homes, leaving 14 million people with nowhere to live.

Rescuers struggled to reach people stranded by rising waters or cut off because roads and bridges were damaged. The army used helicopters to airlift people to safety.

The floods that washed over the land left millions hungry and in danger of catching diseases from the dirty water.

The floods destroyed 8,500 square miles (22,000 sq km) of crops, and 450,000 farm animals were killed.

8 JOHNSTOWN

The Johnstown Flood of 1889 was the deadliest flood in US history. The flood happened after a dam burst, killing 2,209 people.

Johnstown

The Death of a Dam

The area around Johnstown, Pennsylvania, had received a lot of heavy rain, which had filled the reservoir behind the South Fork Dam, 14 miles (23 km) upstream of the town. The dam was built from layers of soil and was not in a good state of repair, even though it held back a large volume of water. The town was warned that the dam might give way, but there had been several false alarms before, so tragically the warnings were ignored.

On the Record

The dam broke on the afternoon of May 31. It released a 30-foot-high (9 m) wall of water, which flowed down the valley toward Johnstown at speeds of up to 20–40 miles (32–64 km) per hour.

In Johnstown, 20 million tons (18 million mt) of water carrying trees, rocks and **debris** crashed into the streets. The flood flattened everything in its path and washed away steel mills, homes, farm animals, and people.

The flood was stopped by a huge stone bridge at the far side of town. This caused water and all of the debris in it, such as locomotives, wood, and human bodies, to back up over the city.

Around 4 square miles (10 square km) of Johnstown were completely destroyed.

Wooden items trapped at the bridge caught fire and killed more people.

7 NORTH SEA

In 1953, a combination of high tides, strong winds, and storm surges caused the North Sea to rise by almost 20 feet (6 m). It broke through flood defenses and caused devastating floods in low-lying parts of the Netherlands, Belgium, and the United Kingdom.

North Sea

Storm Surges

A storm surge happens when an area of low **pressure** and high winds push an unusually high tide toward a coastline. When this water hits low-lying land, it floods the shore. On the night of Saturday, January 31, 1953, and the morning of February 1, 1953, the already high **spring tides** of the North Sea swept ashore. No one was warned it would happen.

On the Record

The floods killed more than 2,000 people: 307 in England, 19 in Scotland, and 1,800 in the Netherlands. There, as much as 50 percent of the land is less than 3 feet (1 m) above **sea level**.

More than 250 square miles (650 sq km) of land were flooded with salty seawater, making it unfit for planting for several years. In the United Kingdom, large areas of East Anglia and the Thames Estuary flooded. In the Netherlands, 10 percent of all farmland was submerged.

This view shows the damage the 1953 floods caused to Zuid-Beveland in the Netherlands.

Today, the River Thames is protected from floods by the Thames Barrier. The Netherlands now has a series of impressive flood defenses.

The floods caused about $74 million worth of damage, about $1.8 billion in today's money.

The flood damaged and destroyed power stations, gasworks, roads, railroads, sewage services, and water services.

6 NORTH INDIA

In June 2013, the mountainous region of Uttarakhand in northern India suffered days of heavy monsoon rains. The rains triggered devastating floods and landslides that killed more than 5,000 people.

North India

Human Impacts

The flood was made worse because of human actions. People had cut down forests in the valleys, so there were fewer tree roots to hold the earth together. Hydroelectric dams across rivers caused water levels in the rivers to rise. There were also many homes and hotels built on riverbanks and in other areas that were likely to flood.

On the Record

The rain was so heavy that 23 inches (59 cm) fell in just two days.

Due to the heavy and persistent rain, a **glacier** in the mountains melted. It triggered flooding in the Mandinkini River.

On June 16–17, 2013, the floods washed away 400 villages, as well as roads, bridges, and other **infrastructure** in 12 of the 13 districts in Uttarakhand.

This house in Kedarnath, Uttarakhand, was destroyed by a landslide following the 2013 floods.

Almost 100,000 pilgrims and tourists visiting Hindu mountain shrines and temples were stranded in the mountain valleys after bridges and roads were destroyed. Some were rescued by helicopter.

5 VENEZUELA

In December 1999, days of torrential rain finally took their toll and caused catastrophic flooding and landslides in the mountainous region of Vargas, in Venezuela. Between 10,000 and 30,000 people were killed in the disaster.

Venezuela

Deadly Debris Flows

The heavy rains washed down the side of the Avila Mountain. The waters dislodged mud, rock, and large boulders. Together they formed deadly debris flows. These stormed down the slopes toward towns and villages below, damaging or destroying everything in their path. Many people living in the area below the mountain were buried under the wet mud or washed into the ocean at the foot of the mountains.

On the Record

In Vargas, several hundred thousand people lived on the narrow strip of coastline at the base of several steep mountains. The floods destroyed a 60-mile (100 km) stretch of the coastline.

This building in Vargas partially collapsed.

The Avila Mountains rise to more than 8,200 feet (2,500 m) above sea level.

The floods and debris flows began late on the night of December 15, and continued until the afternoon of December 16.

An estimated 190,000 people were evacuated, and tens of thousands of people were made homeless.

Telephone, water, electricity, and sewage systems were destroyed or damaged.

Poor families suffered the most, because the torrents of mud and water swept away their lightly constructed homes and **shantytowns**. Entire apartment blocks collapsed.

4 BANGLADESH

During the monsoon season in 1974, heavy rains caused severe flooding in Bangladesh. People died in the floodwaters and from starvation after the floods devastated most of the rice and other crops in the area. In total, the disaster led to the deaths of at least 28,000 people.

Bangladesh

Flood Plains

The monsoon season brings vital rainwater to Bangladesh for growing crops. The problem is that around three-quarters of the country is less than 33 feet (10 m) above sea level. Almost 80 percent of the land is prone to flooding.

On the Record

The monsoon rains caused massive flooding in the Brahmaputra River, leaving around 40 percent of the country underwater.

The people who suffered most were the poor. Their houses collapsed or were submerged underwater. The floods washed away their belongings.

Bangladesh is frequently affected by flooding. This village was completely destroyed by floodwaters during a cyclone.

The flood damaged about 600,000 tons (536,000 mt) of crops. Food prices rose, so poorer people could not afford to eat.

The loss of crops meant many farmworkers could not get jobs harvesting the crops. Without wages, they could not buy food for their families.

3 YANGTZE RIVER

The Yangtze River runs through central and eastern China. It is the longest river in Asia. Over time, the floods in this river have killed many thousands of people. One of the worst occurred in 1998.

Yangtze River

A History of Flooding

Floods are one of the most serious natural disasters in China. During the twentieth century alone, the Yangtze had five disastrous floods. The flood of 1998 was not the deadliest. It killed around 4,000 people. However, it was devastating and record-breaking in other ways. The 1998 flood lasted more than 80 days and was one of the largest ever recorded.

On the Record

To keep the Yangtze River from flooding, the Chinese government built the Three Gorges Dam. Building work had begun in 1994, but was not able to prevent the 1998 flood. However, it did hold back the worst of a flood in 2010.

The 1998 floods began when unusually heavy rains fell from the start of June to the end of August. The rainfall was up to twice as heavy as usual.

To build the Three Gorges Dam, the Chinese government had to remove 1.2 million people from their towns and villages before the land behind the dam was flooded.

The flood destroyed 13 million homes and submerged 38,600 square miles (100,000 sq km) of land.

The flood made around 15 million people homeless.

23

2 GANGES DELTA

The Ganges Delta is an area of low-lying land about 220 miles (355 km) wide along the Bay of Bengal. It is the area where two huge rivers, the Ganges River in India and the Brahmaputra River in Bangladesh, meet the sea. In 1970, the area was hit by terrible floods.

Ganges Delta

Cyclone Storm

Cyclones regularly form over the warm seas of the Bay of Bengal between August and October, when weather in the region is hot. In November 1970, Cyclone Bhola blew in toward the Bay of Bengal. Unfortunately, the shape of the bay helped to funnel the cyclone toward the coastline. A huge storm surge approached the shore. This sudden increase in sea level flooded the delta regions in both India and Bangladesh (known as East Pakistan at the time).

On the Record

Waves from the storm surge that flooded the delta were 26 feet (8 m) high.

Around 500,000 people were killed; most drowned.

Survivors said the water made a roar like thunder as it raced toward them.

Around 85 percent of all homes in the area were destroyed or badly damaged. More than 1 million people were left homeless.

Crops were destroyed and farm animals drowned throughout the region.

This aerial view shows the Ganges-Brahmaputra Delta, the area flooded in 1970.

1 CHINA

The flooding that happened across central China in 1931 was the deadliest natural disaster of the twentieth century. Between July and August that year there was a series of devastating floods when China's three main rivers, the Yangtze, the Yellow, and the Huai, burst their banks.

China

Deadliest Flood

In late summer 1931, there were increasingly heavy rain showers over a lot of central China, and a series of cyclones. The most destructive floods began in July and continued for two months. The death toll from the floods, and subsequent disease and famine, was between 850,000 and 4 million. The floods left more than 80 million people homeless.

On the Record

Many areas were covered in water up to 15 feet (5 m) deep for up to six months.

When the Huai River overflowed into the city of Nanjing, China's capital at that time, millions of people drowned. Many of those who survived later died from diseases such as cholera.

Water broke through the levees containing the Grand Canal and caused more floods. In one area, 20,000 people drowned in their sleep.

The water level rose 53 feet (16 m) in the area now known as Wuhan.

The Yellow River is named for the large amounts of fine yellow sediment that color its water.

WHERE IN THE WORLD?

This map shows the locations of the floods featured in this book.

- North Sea
- Yangtze River
- China
- North India
- Pakistan
- Bangladesh
- Ganges Delta

INDIAN OCEAN

Read the case studies about the Mississippi flood (1927), the number 10 flood in this book, and the flood in China (1931), which is number 1. How do they differ?

What facts can you find in this book to support the argument that human actions can make flood disasters worse?

GLOSSARY

crops Plants grown for food.

cyclones Storms with violent winds and heavy rains in the South Pacific Ocean and Indian Ocean.

dams Barriers built to hold back river waters. Hydroelectric dams are used to make electricity with the power of falling water.

debris Loose waste material.

delta A roughly triangular area of land where slow-moving river waters meet the sea.

evacuate To get away from an area that is dangerous to somewhere that is safe.

glacier A large, very slow-moving river of ice.

hurricanes Storms with violent winds and heavy rains in the Atlantic Ocean or Northeast Pacific Ocean.

infrastructure Structures such as highways and railroads that towns and cities need.

landslides Collapses of masses of earth or rock from mountains or cliffs.

levees Raised walls or banks by a river, canal, or sea designed to keep water from flooding the land.

monsoon Seasonal wind that brings heavy rains in some tropical parts of the world.

plantation A large farm where crops such as bananas are grown.

pollute To make something dirty or poisonous.

pressure The pushing force on the ground caused by the weight of the air. Air pressure depends on temperature and wind.

radar A machine that uses radio waves to detect where objects are.

reservoirs Artificial lakes where water is collected and stored, often behind dams.

satellite Object in space that travels around Earth.

sea level The average height of the ocean's surface.

shantytowns Areas on the edges of cities where poor people live in small, very cheaply built houses.

spring tides Tides in which there is the greatest difference between high and low water. They can be very high and very low.

storm surges Abnormal rises of water generated by hurricanes or other storms.

tributaries Rivers or streams that flow into larger rivers.

tropical The area of Earth around the equator that is hot all year.

FURTHER READING

Books

Baker, John R. *The World's Worst Floods* (World's Worst Natural Disasters). North Mankato, MN: Capstone Press, 2016.

Johnson, Robin. *What Is a Flood?* (Severe Weather Close-Up). New York, NY: Crabtree Publishing Company, 2016.

Perish, Patrick. *Survive a Flood* (Survival Zone). Minneapolis, MN: Bellwether Media Inc., 2016.

Raum, Elizabeth. *Flood!* (Natural Disasters). Mankato, MN: Amicus Publishing, 2016.

Websites

Due to the changing nature of Internet links, PowerKids Press has developed an online list of websites related to the subject of this book. This site is updated regularly. Please use this link to access the list: **www.powerkidslinks.com/nud/floods**

INDEX

B
Bangladesh, 20–21, 24–25, 28
Brahmaputra River, 21, 24

C
China, 22–23, 26–28
clouds, 5
crops, 4, 11, 20–21, 25
Cyclone Bhola, 24
cyclones, 6, 24, 26

D
dams, 7, 12–13, 16, 23
delta, 24–25
disease, 4, 11, 26–27

F
fires, 4, 13
flash floods, 6

G
Ganges Delta, 24–25, 28
Ganges River, 24

H
homes, 4, 9, 11, 13, 16, 19, 23, 25
Huai River, 26–27
hurricanes, 6

I
India, 7, 16–17, 24, 28
Indus River, 10

J
Johnstown, 12–13, 29

L
levees, 8–9, 27

M
Mandinkini River, 17
Mississippi, 8–9, 28–29
monsoon, 7, 10, 16, 20–21
mountains, 17–19

N
Netherlands, 14–15
North Sea, 14–15, 28

P
Pakistan, 10–11, 28
plantation, 9
power lines, 4

R
radar, 5
rain, 5–8, 10, 12, 16–18, 20–21, 23, 26
rescued, 17
reservoirs, 7, 12
river, 4, 6, 8, 10, 15–17, 21–24, 26–28
River Thames, 15

S
storm surges, 14, 24–25

T
tides, 14

U
United Kingdom, 7, 14–15
United States, 8–9

V
Venezuela, 18–19, 29

Y
Yangtze River, 22–23, 26, 28
Yellow River, 26

Edison Twp. Free Public Library
340 Plainfield Ave.
Edison, New Jersey 08817

JUN 27 2017